# THE SECRETS OF HAPPY PARENTING

# The Secrets of Happy Parenting

Apostle Dr. Victor Adewusi

Apostle Dr. Victor Adewusi Foundation

# Contents

*Foreword*    vii
*Introduction*    xi

| | | |
|---|---|---|
| 1 | The Best Approach | 1 |
| 2 | Developmental Milestones | 5 |
| 3 | The Essential Duties of a True Parent | 8 |
| 4 | Child Development | 10 |
| 5 | Proper Parenting Roles | 13 |
| 6 | Parenting - The Biblical Perspective | 24 |
| 7 | Do You Want to be a Good Parent? | 30 |
| 8 | The 10 Major Ingredients | 40 |
| 9 | Avoid These as Much as Possible | 45 |
| 10 | Special Biblical References on Child Training & Parenting | 50 |
| 11 | Children and Their Parents | 54 |

*Conclusion*    59
*A Sinner's Prayer*    61
*About the Author*    63

Copyright © 2022 by Aposle Dr. Victor Adewusi

All rights reserved. No part of this book may be used or reproduced by any means, graphics, electronic, or mechanical, including photocopying, recording, taping or by any information storage retrieval system without the author's written permission except in cases of brief quotations embodied in critical articles and reviews.

Scripture quotations marked NLT are taken from the New Living Translation. Copyright © 1996, 2004, 2007 by Tyndale House Foundation. Used by permission of Tyndale House Publishers, Inc., Carol Stream, Illinois 60188. All rights reserved.

Author: Apostle Dr. Victor Adewusi

ISBN: 978-1-989099-14-8 (hardcover)
ISBN: 978-1-989099-15-5 (ebook)

First Printing, 2022

# *Foreword*

One day as a kid, I was watching a program on the television, and this advertisement came up about my favourite chocolate. I was fully engrossed watching it and wishing internally to eat some at that moment, my father walked into the room and offered me a piece of that same chocolate. I knew he was an exceptionally gifted spiritual leader, but I was shocked as to just how he had one with him at that moment. He told me that he always endeavours to have that chocolate with him because he knows it's my favourite. This shows that parenting goes beyond just caring for your child and being aware and passionate about things that they love.

My father had both biological and non-biological children, and I am the last born of his biological children. After having four children, you would think he would be slack or tired in his parenting principles when I was growing up; however, it was the opposite. I am a wife and mom to two amazingly energetic and loving boys. His love, passion, discipline, and principles have been a driving force to where I am today and a sound of reasoning in my own parenting journey.

I remember calling my dad at almost 2 am Nigerian time, informing him of my scholarship to study Master of clinical practice (Nursing) at Massey University in New Zealand. I heard him stand up from the bed and roll on the floor with so much excitement in his voice, glorifying God. You see, this would be my 4th degree, so it was by no means my first education, but my father always found a reason to demonstrate love and support to his children.

Today, as I have the honour to write this foreword to one of dad's five books - "The Secrets of Happy Parenting" I share words that I believe should encourage every parent or carer to read this book and learn the tried and tested secrets from my father's parenting style.

I kept having several flashbacks of my childhood while reading this book. Growing up, some events or reactions made sense when they were happening; however, this book finally gave me insight into why daddy had taken certain actions. In the book, daddy wrote about responding to your children's needs in a predictable manner. I remember numerous scenarios where someone would report my actions to daddy, and instead of immediately taking sides, he would always ask me to explain my side of the accusations before giving a constructive response or action. This confidence in my dad's predictable response assured me that he was an objective parent and I would not be disciplined unjustly.

There is a remarkable degree of wisdom that every parent needs to care for their child(ren) effectively. It is a 'learn-as-you-go' skill that can not really be taught; however, my dad seemed to have mastered it quite well. In the book, he noted that "Good parenting involves a style that considers children's age and stage of development." For some reason, as a child, I was fond of unconsciously leaving my mouth open without speaking. Instead of leaving me to keep embarrassing myself, my dad coined an abbreviation - PTT - put them together. Therefore, anytime we were outside and I had my mouth opened, my dad would confidently say PTT, and I would immediately realize my mouth was open and close it.

My dad had numerous personal and work responsibilities, yet he was involved in the day-to-day activities of all his children. Even during financial difficulties, he still ensured that we had the best education and recreational activities. Some of our playtime growing up was studying the map of the world! Little did we know, he was setting us up to represent the family in different parts of the world. I can confidently say that his children are successful and performing exploits in various parts of the world.

Parenting is not a one size fits all situation, and I, therefore, believe that children should be cared for based on their personalities and capabilities. However, it is crucial to know and understand the fundamentals of what or who a parent is. There is no other person I would rather learn from than my dad.

Apostle Dr. Victor Adekunle Adewusi, my dad of blessed memory, passed away on the 21st of August, 2021. He wrote the manuscript of this book in December 2020 when he was on holiday in Canada to visit his son and the family. Instead of enjoying his vacation, he was determined to finish writing this book and four others as he felt the leading of the Holy Spirit to do so. Little did we know that he would pass on to eternal glory a few months later. I had the blessed opportunity to learn first-hand parenting secrets from this great man, which is helping me be a great wife and mom to my children. Therefore, I am so glad that through the pages of this book, others would also have the opportunity to learn the secrets of happy parenting and, albeit, secrets of a great family.

**Florence Edeigba**

# *Introduction*

Many people, including my biological and spiritual children, have urged me to write a book on parenting. The same requests have been coming in from most of my church members and most of the parents that I have counselled over the years. I hope my conscious efforts will satisfy their desires and curiosity!

A parent is a father or a mother who begets or gives birth to, nurtures and raises a child, or a relative who plays the role of a guardian.

Parenting involves a lot of attention from either the birth parent or the guardian; and has these essential components, namely:

1. **Care:** protects children from harm and encompasses promoting emotional and physical health.
2. **Control:** involves setting and enforcing boundaries to ensure the safety of children and others in ever-widening areas of activity.

The importance of parenting arises from its role as a buffer against adversity such as poverty, delinquent influences, or a mediator of damage. Parenting usually involves biological parents, but it is not solely limited to them since carers, teachers, nurses and others also fulfill parenting tasks in the lives of children. It also involves optimizing children's potential and maximizing the opportunities for using it. It is a complex and demanding job.

Most parents care for their children, sometimes even against great odds. The motivation to nurture and protect children is not inborn in humans but is acquired and shaped through past experiences and current circumstances. It is good to have a parenting society where all citizens recognize their shared rights and responsibilities for giving and receiving care, control, and development, particularly to the needy, among whom children are the most prominent. Parenting is all about using the family's unique passions, values and beliefs to guide parenting decisions that lead to raising good children and simultaneously building a very warm and close bond with them.

Since we don't have a particular "parenting script" due to family differences, any unique act of parenting involves giving proper directions and imposing laid down systems of behaviour on the children. Whatever method is adopted, the ultimate objective of every good parent is to produce happy and wonderful children. Modern parents are always open to learning about new and better ways to parent their children by creating a positive and close connection with their children. Parents are supposed to impose rules, use discipline, set limits and standards, and establish and follow through with very strict consequences. While doing so, they must hold the children accountable for their behaviours and teach them morals and values that are acceptable to society. Parents basically provide guidance that helps their children positively grow, change, and become glaringly mature in almost all aspects of human endeavour.

Proper parenting involves taking care of the child's basic needs, which include, but are not limited to, feeding, medical care, shelter, clothing, and proper education while demonstrating love, understanding, acceptance, and availability whenever support is needed. It is always good to listen to them with rapt attention. As simple as it may seem or look, parenting is somehow a complex matter. At times, children can feel or think that you are being very harsh, too strict or even wicked, whereas all you are doing as a parent is shaping them and robustly preparing them for a better and greater tomorrow. Whatever the case may be, parents should do the best that they can do to lay a very solid foundation upon which children could lay a solid structure that would give them a competitive edge among their peers in society.

# 1

# The Best Approach

It is always good to listen to our children, show love, and constantly realize that we were once like them. We should create time for them and show interest in what they are doing in their daily activities. We must encourage them in their passions through our words and actions. Based on these two actions, we either communicate to them that they are loved and accepted or hated and despised, depending on how they view or analyze how we deal with them.

As parents, we nurture our children or wards by allowing them to feel good about themselves and letting them know that they are worthy of being loved and cared for. This gives them the confidence that their needs will be met, the assurance that their ideas, feelings, and needs are important and that they will be understood. Once we value them for who they are, it helps to build their self-esteem. The ability to face challenges and tackle difficult issues in life becomes greater and stronger as children grow since they are very sure that we, as parents, will support them. Once they receive the anticipated support, they are also able to give back to others as a sign of their empathy. Hence, the strong foundation for an early parent-child relationship is solidified through early bonding of understanding the child's emotional needs.

Whenever we give too much nurture to our children, we may be overly protective and too responsive to their needs and become too involved in their lives. In this process, children become lackadaisical about their future; they do not feel like learning skills to give them a guaranteed future, and talkless of considering other people's needs. Alternatively, when parents are not nurturing enough, they become emotionally distant and not adequately involved in the children's lives. The end result is apathy by the children; they do not learn to trust other people because they no longer feel loved or supported.

A major aspect of parenting is forming a "structure role" because every other function will be gradually built on them. The role involves giving direction, imposing rules, using discipline, setting attainable limits, establishing and following through with stern consequences, holding them accountable for their behaviour and teaching them morals/ethical values, especially as they affect the family background. Parents are expected to provide guidance that helps children change, grow, and mature. Thus, responsible behaviour is taught and expected according to the children's maturity levels. Parents must expect a change in behaviour and increased growth, maturity and ability under the structure role. This "structure role" has a lot of benefits for the children. They feel a sense of safety knowing that rules will always be in place whenever they fail to control their impulses their parents will be there to help regulate those impulses, while guiding and monitoring their well-being effectively. It is expected that they will learn to tolerate a reasonable amount of frustration and disappointment whenever things don't go as expected; they become less egocentric. They learn from their mistakes and gain experience while making decisions. This cultivates responsible behaviour that gives them the self-confidence they need to become self-sufficient and capable of learning the required skills to become independent. As the nurturing process continues, parents must internalize the family's rules and morals. Parents must endeavour not to provide too much structure as much as possible. Doing so could reflect that the parent is rigid and harsh regarding enforcing discipline, whereas children don't always learn to think for themselves, making them passive or rebellious. On the other hand, when too little structure is given, parents' expectations and rules can be unclear, distorted and inconsistent, thereby confusing the children. In that light, they won't feel they will be protected, and lack accountability for their actions.

In addition to finding a balance on each side of caring or control, parents must balance how and when to nurture their children and how and when to provide a structure of discipline and its limits. Providing only the nurturing or caring piece without structure or limits or holding them accountable for their actions could spoil them, making them unappreciative, self-centred, and void of independence. That could portray the parents as weak, driving them to over-indulge in a way.

As children develop from infants to teens, then to adulthood, they go through a series of physical, intellectual, emotional and social developmental stages that are important to all aspects of their personhood. The proper role of the parent is to provide overall encouragement, support and access to all the activities that will enable the child to master key developmental tasks. A parent is their child's first and best teacher and should remain at that level throughout their life.

The early years of a child's life are very crucial for their health and development. A healthy environment means that children of all abilities, including those with special health care needs, can grow up where their social, emotional and educational needs are duly met. Also, having a safe and loving home and spending time with the family, such as playing, singing, reading, and talking, are essential roles to be played by every caring parent. Also, proper nutrition, regular exercise and having enough sleep in a conducive environment can make a huge difference in the life and upbringing of the child.

Parenting takes many different forms. However, positive parenting practices work well across diverse families and settings. This form of parenting provides the care that children need to be happy, healthy, grow and develop well. I have tried the following steps during the process of bringing up our children, and it has worked for us tremendously:

1. **Responding to their needs in a predictable manner**
2. **Showing warmth and sensitivity**
3. **Having routines and household rules**
4. **Sharing books and talking with the children as if we are age mates**
5. **Supporting their health and safety needs**
6. **Using appropriate discipline without harshness**

I must, however, mention that I did not spare the rod when necessary, but I don't think that practice is still in vogue! It, however, has its merits and demerits, depending on the parent, family, and behavioural tendencies of the children. If the parent is not a beast and the children do not display any animalistic tendencies, there is no reason for applying the "cane" or the rod. Any parent who sees the above six steps as practical and wishes to adopt them can help their children stay healthy, safe, and remain successful in many areas of human endeavour-emotional, behavioural, cognitive and social.

# 2

# Developmental Milestones

Nurturing a child is a step-by-step process. After discussing some of a parent's essential duties as much as possible, it is also pertinent to discuss some of the developmental milestones. Skills such as taking the first step, smiling for the first time and waving "bye-bye" are referred to as developmental milestones and need to be touched as briefly as possible.

Children reach their milestones in how they play, learn, speak, behave, and more, such as crawling and walking. They develop at their own pace, making it sometimes impossible to tell exactly when a child will learn a particular skill. But the developmental milestones give an overall idea of the changes to expect as a child gets older. Some children begin to crawl, talk and walk faster than their age mates, which was the experience I had with my wife while our children were trying to get their acts together.

As a parent, we are expected to know our children best. If our children are not meeting the milestones for their age, or if we think there could be a problem with the child's development, it is better to usually consult a medical practitioner or begin to pray for them. We did this on most occasions, perhaps because of our positions and backgrounds; I am an Apostle, while my wife is a Lady Evangelist!

A child's growth and development can safely be categorized into four periods:

1. **Infancy**
2. **Preschool years**
3. **Middle school (childhood years)**
4. **Adolescence**

Soon after birth, an infant is expected to use about 5%-10% of their birth weight. But around and from 2 weeks upward, an infant should begin to gain weight and grow quickly. By 4-6 months, it should be double their birth weight, and during the second half of the first year of life, growth is not as rapid. But between 1 and 2, a toddler will gain only about 2.2 kilograms and will remain at about the same 2.2 kilograms per year between ages 2-5.

Between ages 2-10 years, a child will grow steadily, with a final growth spurt beginning at the start of puberty, between ages 9-15 years. The child's nutrients need to correspond with these changes in growth rates. An infant needs more calories in relation to size than a preschooler or school-age child needs. Nutrient needs increase again as a child gets close to adolescence. A healthy child would follow an individual growth curve, as we observed from our children. However, the nutrient intake may differ for each child (we gave our children the same nutrient, but I don't think it's still in the market!) Parents must, however, provide a diet with a wide variety of foods that are suited to the child's age.

Healthy eating habits should begin during infancy, as it will help to prevent diseases such as high blood pressure and obesity.

Poor nutrition can cause problems with a child's intellectual development, they may experience fatigue and the inability to learn at school. Children are also more likely to get sick and miss school. As parents, we must ensure that our children do not miss breakfast, as this is very important so that they are not tired and unmotivated. Experience has shown a positive correlation between daily nutritious breakfast and learning. I have decided to mention this aspect in this book since it is one of the attributes of good parenting. Parenting is not just giving birth to a child. Taking proper care of them from infancy to adolescence and into a full grown adult growth is the ultimate goal, and I sincerely thank God that my wife and I succeeded in achieving that set goal.

Again, suppose a parent is too rigid with rules, strict procedures and limits without a strong, loving relationship. The obvious thing for the child to do is to become resentful, and uncooperative without feeling much remorse as a result of feeling unloved. Once a child realizes that punishment is the typical outcome for their behaviour, they can resolve to hide their mistakes and weaknesses from their parents, which could ultimately force unsuspecting parents to miss golden opportunities to influence their children's behaviour and choices. Therefore, the most advisable thing is for parents to consciously provide both nurture (caring, loving relationship) and structure (setting limits for discipline, moral standards, etc.). A strong and discerning parent should be able to constantly determine which side of the scale the weight should tilt more. However, healthy parenting MUST ensure that the scale does not become too weighed on either side and make the necessary adjustments if it does to reflect the children's positive development.

# 3

# The Essential Duties of a True Parent

It is very apt to properly define and explain the meaning of parenting before moving ahead.

It is the process of raising children (or a child) and providing them with protection and care to ensure their healthy development into adulthood. It is also the process of promoting and supporting a child's physical, emotional, social, and intellectual development from infancy to adulthood. Parenting refers to the intricacies of raising a child and NOT exclusively for a biological relationship. In some cases, orphaned or abandoned children receive parental care from other blood relatives, while others may be raised in foster care or an orphanage. While there are many types of parenting, it is ideal to be in the group of good parenting.

Good parenting involves a great deal of consistency and routine, which gives children a sense of control. It also involves a style that considers children's age and stage of development and focuses on developing independence in children, so redundancy becomes the aim for parents.

Parenting has two essential components:

1. **Care:** protects children from harm. It also encompasses promoting emotional and physical health
2. **Control:** involves setting and enforcing boundaries to ensure the safety of children and others in ever-widening areas of life

A parent is a person who raises and cares for another person. Since there are different types of parents (such as step-parents, grandparents, legal guardians, etc.), being a parent does not necessarily imply a biological connection or that their genetics were passed on to the child.

As mentioned earlier, there is both good and bad parenting. Bad parenting involves but is NOT limited to neglect and abuse, be it physical, emotional or sexual abuse by a parent to their child or ward.

A good parent's job involves raising a child to be the best person they can be and is a huge responsibility that warrants glaring patience, love and understanding. A good parent is expected to reflect the following basic qualities:

1. **Caretaker:** physically and emotionally putting his essential needs before yours
2. **Provider:** the child must always be well-fed while ensuring that they are healthy and well clothed
3. **Protector:** the child must be safe at all times without any consistent threat to their security
4. **Beloved:** the love that a parent has for their child is incomparable because the child must be seen as the parent's "everything"
5. **Counsellor & Confidant:** since a parent is expected to have his child's best interests at heart, he is in a good position to give sound advice to ensure that such a child achieves their full potential in life

# 4

# Child Development

Remember, child development refers to the sequence of physical, language, thought, and emotional changes in a child, from birth to the beginning of adulthood. During this process, a child progresses from dependency on their parents/guardians to increasing independence.

Child development is strongly influenced by genetic factors, that is, genes passed to them from their parents and events during prenatal life. It is also influenced by environmental factors and the child's learning capacity. It can be actively enhanced through targeted therapeutic intervention and the "just right" home-based practice recommended by occupational and speech therapists. We, however, did not have any reason to go to that extent concerning any of our children.

Child development also covers the full scope of skills that a child masters over their life span and includes growth in the following:

1. **Cognition:** the ability to learn and solve problems
2. **Social interaction and emotional regulation:** interacting with others and mastering self-control

3. **Speech and language:** understanding and using language, reading and communicating
4. **Physical skills:** motor movement
5. **Sensory awareness:** the registration of sensory information for use. Observing and monitoring a child's development is a wonderful tool to ensure that children meet their "milestones" that act as valuable guidelines for ideal development. Consciously checking a child's developmental progress at particular age markers against these arbitrary time frames allows a "check-in" to ensure that the child is roughly "on track" for their age.
6. **Learning:** The parent has a lot to teach a child. This could include how to walk, the difference between right and wrong, how to conduct oneself in social gatherings or settings, the proper mode of dressing and moral standards.
7. **Parents are seen as role models:** 99.5% of children see their parents as small or semi-gods and imitate their parent's behaviour in almost all facets. Therefore, parents should do their best to display proper human ethics in all they do in the presence of their children.

Preparing children for adulthood is the primary role of a parent. And from that perspective, a parent is not raising a child but an adult. Daily, parents make choices and act deliberately to help shape their children into people with good character, respect, a sense of responsibility, motivation, and skills to help them become successful as kids and adults, although it can be laced with difficult times. However, when a parent's relationship is rooted in love, a bond is created that remains strong and can bring the parents together anytime disagreements and arguments occur. Loving our children nurtures them and helps them thrive. A hug, a kiss on the head, laughter, and the joy of being together is perhaps the best description of the meaning of parenting. Proper parenting promotes the child's mental, linguistic and emotional development; it helps the child to exhibit optimistic and confident social behaviours. Healthy parent involvement and intervention in the child's daily life lay the foundation for healthy and enriching adult life.

The parent-child relationship nurtures the child's physical, emotional, and social development. It is a unique bond that every child and parent can enjoy and nurture! This type of relationship lays the foundation for the child's personality, life choices and overall behaviour. It can also affect the strength of their social, physical, mental and emotional health. There are many benefits of good parenting, viz:

1. Young children who grow with a secure and healthy attachment to their parents stand a better chance of developing happy and content relationships with others in their life.
2. A child who has a secure relationship with their parent learns to regulate emotions under stress and in difficult situations.
3. It promotes the child's mental, linguistic and emotional development.
4. It helps the child exhibit optimistic and confident social behaviours.
5. Healthy parent involvement and intervention in the child's daily life lay the foundation for better social and academic skills.
6. A secure attachment leads to healthy social, emotional, cognitive and motivational development. Children also gain strong problem-solving skills when they have a positive relationship with their parents.

# 5

# Proper Parenting Roles

The proper role of the parent is to provide encouragement, support and access to activities that enable the child to master key development tasks; and to remain the best teacher throughout the child's life.

The duties and responsibilities of a good parent are multifaceted, but they can be broken down into the six significant roles below:

1. **To protect the child from harm**
2. **To provide the child with food, clothing and shelter**
3. **To support the child financially**
4. **To provide safety, supervision and control/monitoring**
5. **To provide mental care**
6. **To provide education**

Apart from the above, a good and caring parent is expected to provide the child with very sound moral and spiritual guidance, ensure uprightness, inculcate honesty, integrity, self-discipline, self-reliance, industry, and bring out the best in them concerning their skills towards a sustainable future. The parent is also expected to inspire the child and teach the need to always comply with the duties of citizenship and how to manage their resources with particular reference to investments.

Parents are supposed to keep their children in their company, either directly or by monitoring them wherever they are, to:

1. Support and instruct them by right precepts and good/morals, such as providing for their upbringing in keeping up with their needs.
2. Show them love and affection, advice and counsel, companionship and understanding.
3. Furnish them with good and wholesome educational requirements; supervise their overall activities, recreation and association with others. Protect them from bad company and prevent them from copying untoward habits that are detrimental to their health, studies and morals.
4. Represent them in all matters that affect their interests, and demand respect and obedience from them.
5. Impose discipline on them as required under any legal circumstances and perform other duties legitimately as a good and caring parent.

Parents are responsible for meeting and catering to the overall needs of the family and children according to their capability. Parents are legally expected to care for and raise a child in a responsible manner. They also have the right to access any official record directly relating to the children under their parental responsibilities. Parents are supposed to be liable for the child's overall maintenance until they reach the age of maturity, which varies from one country to another. Some countries' age of maturity is 18, while others are 21, depending on the country's policy and legal framework.

A child's legal parents are the mother and the father. The mother is the woman who gave birth to the child, who could be a woman that became pregnant naturally or became conceived using a donor egg. The woman might have also adopted the child legally to become the legitimate mother. Similarly, the father is the mother's husband or a registered partner at the time of the child's birth unless the child's paternity is denied. The man who has acknowledged or adopted the child or has been declared the child's father by a court is legally entitled to be referred to as the man who fathered the child.

A good and caring parent must ensure that their children are always happy. This may not be so at all times, but this is where the ingenuity of a parent comes in handy. When a parent sets limits or establishes consequences, they may not like it initially. Our children are now beginning to realize that we were, after all, not "wicked" towards them during their upbringing. But that is how life is; everybody wants everything to "go easy"! Parents are not supposed to make decisions based on their children's expectations or what they like. No. Strict and strongly enforced rules or guidelines are not expected to be admired or tolerated by the children. Instead, parents should make the best decisions for themselves and the family, then follow through with them.

At times, it is better to run the family like a business entity. Parents should see themselves as the chief executive officer (CEO). Why? A CEO who wants to make a profit, and keep the company running, is just like a parent who wants to keep their children on their toes. The parent must learn how to set emotions aside as objectively as possible.

They must also ignore the feelings of guilt as long as they know what they are doing and enforcing is in the best interests of the child. One could seek or ask for advice, but ultimately the parent knows their family best and knows what is suitable for them. With this in mind, it is okay to forget or discount the echo of advice from others in the back of their head and constantly remember that they need to do what is best for their family.

Despite what many think or believe, parenting is NOT a popularity contest, whether in the family or the community. A parent must ensure to make provisions for whatever aids in a child excelling wherever they are or find themselves, either now or in the foreseeable future. Parents must realize that their children are not puppets, and it is impossible to control all of their movements or everything they say, especially outside of the home! Children have their own free will and act on them based on their own accord, oftentimes in self-interest. So instead of controlling children, we can influence them by the limits we set and the consequences we establish. Remember the popular English idiom that says, "You can lead a horse to the water yet cannot make it drink, but you can make it thirsty!"

Parents are not supposed to do everything for the children; whatever they are capable of doing themselves should not be done for them. We can only show, tell or demonstrate how some things should be carried out or become actualized. It is good for them to "struggle" at times, but it's far better to give them increasing levels of responsibility. Parents must not see themselves as the super-hero. Meaning that, instead of focusing on or deliberately addressing every behaviour issue or adhering to a perfect schedule on a daily basis, parents should just endeavour to address the essential targets and realize that they may have to let some more minor things go once in a while.

As parents, we should bear in mind that if our child does not get angry with us every once in a while, we are NOT doing our job effectively because not all instructions or advice given to them is expected to go down well! Our explanations should not be lengthy but brief to avoid ambiguity. Phrases such as "it's not safe"; "don't touch it"; "its not your responsibility"; "it will hurt you"; or "stop it" are all far better ways of dishing out instructions to them instead of adopting long speeches to deal with them.

Parents should teach the child age-appropriate skills that allow them to become more and more independent. Why? A time will come when the parent is not around and the child needs to carry out tasks such as tying their shoes, writing their name and learning to cope when someone teases him; with more advanced tasks over time. A child must know how to type a paper, say "No" to drugs, drive a car (my children forced themselves to learn without our knowledge!) and fill out a job application paper. We must allow them to realize that their level of responsibility will continue to grow.

As mentioned at the beginning of this book, parents must set limits, and check for any inappropriate behaviour and should be responsible for holding their children accountable for their behaviour and actions. Sometimes, parenting is a bit of a roller coaster that parents ride whether they like it or not. Children can sometimes miss the mark and other times get it perfectly right; but regardless of any negative outcome, parents should always find positive ways to cope and help the child. Parenting is a perpetual balancing act where they must always strive to find that balance between doing too much and doing too little, or giving consequences that are not too harsh but not too soft in any approach. Furthermore, parenting can even look like a circus sometimes, in the sense that there could be several balancing acts going on simultaneously!

Parents must always admit that their child is unique by every standard because they know them better than anyone else in the world. They will constantly receive input, no matter how obvious or subtle, from their environment, about how they should train or handle their child. This is why they must always apply their initiatives at all times to be in the best overall interest of the child. The best goal is for every parent to carry out the onerous assignment of parenting with love and affection.

There is a strong link between what parents know about parenting and child development and how they behave with their children. Parents with more knowledge are more likely to engage in positive parenting practices, whereas those with limited knowledge are at a greater risk of negative parenting behaviours.

Parental involvement helps to excite teaching outside the classroom, creates a more positive experience for children, and helps children perform better when in school. This connection is a key component of a child's development in supporting further learning.

Good parenting skills and a supportive home learning environment are positively associated with children's early achievements and well-being. Thus, interventions to improve the quality of home and family life can increase social mobility.

As much as possible, and where practicable, it is always better for a child to live with both parents. Having the two parents under the same roof in a child's life is essential because they both play very distinct and important roles in the psychological and emotional development of the child. And being a responsible parent means providing love, affection and authority in both the good and bad times.

Parenting takes years of hard work. Even then, we all make mistakes because parenting tests us on every level; emotionally, physically, financially and even spiritually; that is why good parenting rarely comes naturally. Parents with a healthy sense of humour are the most popular adults to look out for. Their kids usually enjoy bringing their friends to the house. Displaying good humour with the children encourages open and unrestrained family dialogue and provides great relief from life's stressors. It makes family time more fun, whereas parents who suffer from humour deficient disorder are real downers and tend to drag their children down in the dumps with them. Flexible parents tend to be open-minded and easy-going because they resolve disagreements smoothly and never engage in shouting matches. We should always realize that children are naturally defiant. Inflexible parents increase defiance and rebelliousness in their children, which tends to escalate conflicts. We should thus recognize our child's right to have a voice in family decisions and matters. That is why, as we usually do in our family, it is better to hold a family meeting before making rules whereby we engage the children in dialogue. The method we usually adopt as being flexible does not mean that our children can do whatever they like and get away with it. Many parents fail to realize that quality listening soothes children better than any couple or recommendations and fulfills two crucial childhood needs: the need to feel understood and the need to be validated.

Over the years, I have discovered that children absorb ten percent of what their parents say and ninety percent of what they do. Therefore, being the person we want our children to be is the most powerful parenting choice a parent can make. Whether we like it or not, children develop personal values and a life philosophy that is based on their parent's choices. Children are born with an innate drive to define themselves and develop their unique strengths and talents. From their first steps to driving a car, they want to stubbornly do things on their own. Good parents nurture independence, foster personal responsibility and encourage self-reliance. Parents should teach their children healthy boundaries in dealing with people by letting them know how to honour and respect the physical and emotional space between people; they lay the foundation for good habits that can last a lifetime. They also nourish confidence by reducing fears and anxieties in children.

Parents should encourage their children to engage in altruistic activities. They learn to see the world beyond their own needs and wants and become skilled at counting their blessings. Helping others is the best antidote for self-centred or arrogant children because it awakens their humanity, inspires greater empathy and kindness, and expands their social views. Good parents are always quick to offer academic support and cultivate solid study habits in their children as early as possible. Once poor study habits take root in a child's life, it is always difficult to reverse them. Parents must ensure that their children are used to working hard so that they won't give up easily when school assignments become more difficult. Teenagers store up a lot of tension in their bodies and need physical outlets to relieve it. Children focus better, relate better, and sleep better with less stored-up tension. They have more self-control, and if they engage in team sports or martial arts, they will get the added benefit of developing more confidence and better social skills. Creating outlets such as drawing, playing an instrument, writing, meditation, or even yoga are also wonderful ways for children to learn how to soothe themselves and calm their minds. Most children inherit eating habits from their parents, so paying attention to what the family consumes at home is essential. Early childhood eating habits leave imprints that rarely fade. Hence, it is advisable to give our children better food choices because in doing so, a parent is unconsciously laying the foundation for health and wellness that the children will carry with them into adulthood!

Parenting and child development go hand in hand. Parents play the most critical role in the overall development of their children. It is the proper guidance of parents that develops the child's character. Parenting is an ongoing job and is not something we can get away from because even in adulthood, children will need their parents from time to time. Thus, the role of parents in child development is responsive, responsible and never-ending. It governs the responses, actions, thinking and decision-making of a child.

When children are growing up, positive parenting improves their cognitive, social and problem-solving skills. Positive parenting also affects their responses and helps them become better humans. It is all about recognizing problems, handling all situations well, and picking up discipline traits such as time management and effective problem-solving through simple routines at home. Our children observe spousal interaction and how arguments or disputes are settled in the family. It teaches them a variety of good values that are imbibed and crucial to growing up. The child learns how to have healthy social interactions with others, play to a common goal with others, and choose the right friends. As a child learns the importance of health, they grow to know the essence of having a balanced diet and regular exercise. A healthy parenting style can help a child learn innovatively, accept failures and overcome feedback, and also teaches them the award-and-punishment concept of life. It ultimately governs their response to stimuli, thus moulding their minds.

The onerous ability to understand religion, the paramount role of right from wrong, being empathetic, having the correct ethical values, valuing one's parents, and strengthening goal-setting, liberates the free spirit in children. Teaching the children to be more accepting and to believe in the greater good can help them gain a sense of purpose. It is also relevant NOT to force them to accept or choose a particular religion but to make a choice themselves.

Children naturally turn to the father to play and the mother if they sense stress or fear. The role of a father in child development is very crucial because children will always look up to their father for motivation. Also, the role of a mother in child development has moved on and is not restricted to nurturing and caretaking alone. From that first touch and look too many years later, a parent is responsible for making the tiny infant into a responsible and caring well-grown adult.

A good, caring and responsible parent is expected to effectively deal with his child in the following ways:

1. **Be positive:** Children can easily sense negativity or danger within their environment. No matter how young the child may be, parents should discuss their problems with their children and how to handle them. We must also encourage the children to

participate with us as parents in different household tasks. We must teach them how to be creative and solve problems with a positive attitude.

2. **Be sensitive to the child's needs:** Irrespective of how small the child's needs are, understanding and fulfilling them is very important to help the child realize that the parent is there for him at all times and that his needs never go unheard.

3. **Be emotionally present:** Open encouragement and love yield good fruits only when they are well cultivated, worked on, nurtured and pruned. We must show children that they are loved all the time and must always be there for them, whatever the situation.

4. **Communicate effectively:** Parents must learn to converse with their children and listen to what they are saying before jumping to conclusions. In every conversation, parents should think from their child's perspective and allow them to express themselves. Positive feedback is always better than negative blame.

5. **Be affectionate:** Children pick up what they see/hear at home. To a child, using harsh words, quarrelling loudly, constantly fighting, incorporating bad habits, and swearing feels absolutely normal if he sees the same at home.

6. **Set routines for play, eating & sleep:** A good routine can help to develop good habits for the future. If the parent sticks to a fixed routine, eats and sleeps on time, and refrains from watching the television during meals, the child will also pick up these lessons and follow them as a routine.

7. **Regular family outings:** Since the family that eats and prays together stays together, parents should encourage their children to eat together at the dining table because that will show them the essence of togetherness and cohesion within the family.

8. **Always find time to talk with your child at all times:** Whether we believe it or not, hard work gives immense satisfaction. The reward for every parent is seeing their child deal with

problems effectively, handle financial matters responsibly, and socialize well with others. However tired parents may be, they must find time to have a chat with their children in order for them to cultivate this habit when they grow into adulthood.

9. **Build trust, love & fair play in relationships:** Parents should be openly fair in dealing with siblings whenever a dispute needs to be settled among them. This same approach when they become grown up in future.
10. **Show honesty & uprightness:** Parents must ensure that children value honesty and uprightness when it concerns matters that involve relationships, money or financial matters. They must be taught the essence of speaking the truth and a sense of responsibility.
11. **Show love & total support:** If the child fails at something, the parent must try to know the reason before he is rebuked. We should let him know that making mistakes is normal and does not reduce the love between people.

# 6

# Parenting - The Biblical Perspective

In order to sincerely appreciate the role of parenting, I have decided to devote an entire chapter of this book to the Biblical approach to our discussion.

Proverbs 22:6 says, *"Train up a child in the way he should go, and when he is old, he will not depart from it."*

The responsibility of parenting is rooted in marriage; where a man and a woman are joined together to establish a godly home where children can be raised and nurtured for a fruitful life. According to Apostle Paul in his letter to the people of Ephesus (Ephesians), 5:31-32, he says, *"For this reason, a man shall leave his father and mother and be joined to his wife, and the two shall become one flesh. This is a great mystery, but I speak concerning Christ and the Church."*

It is quite evident that apart from marriage, and based on Genesis 1:26-28, God's foremost instruction to man gave birth to the role of a parent. It says, "Then God said *"Let us make man in Our image, according to Our likeness; let them have dominion over the fish of the sea, over the birds of the air; and over the cattle; over all the earth and over every creeping thing that creeps on the earth. So God created man in His image; in the Image of God He created him; male and female He created them. Then God blessed them, and God said to them, Be fruitful and multiply; fill the earth and subdue it; have dominion over the fish of the sea, over the birds of the air; and over every living thing that moves on the earth."*

According to Genesis 5:1-3, Adam and Eve were the first and legitimate couple who fulfilled the mandate of marriage and parenting. They produced children in their own "image and likeness" according to the instruction of God, which remains till today. Based on Genesis 1:26-28, we can see that God expects man to be fruitful, multiply, and fill the earth. Therefore, it is ultimately safe to conclude that God's expectations according to parenting are as follows:

1. **For man to reproduce the NATURE of the parent in the child**
2. **For man to reproduce the BEHAVIOUR of the parent in the child**
3. **For man to reproduce the CHARACTER of the parent in the child**

In other words, the nature, behaviour and character of the parent should be clearly reflected in the life of the child as a result of the parents' conscious efforts. The relationship between God and Jesus Christ is the perfect example of parenting, which all parents must try to emulate and copy. But, is it practical? Yes, indeed it is. According to the book of Colossians 1:15, *"He (Jesus Christ) is the image of the invisible God, the firstborn over all creation."* The Bible supports parenting as reflected in the following scriptures:

1. **Deuteronomy 6:6-7** - "And these words which I command you today shall be in your heart. You shall teach them diligently to your children and shall talk of them when you sit in your house, when you walk by the way, when you lie down, and when you rise up."
2. **Ephesians 6:4** - "And you, fathers, do not provoke your children to wrath, but bring them up in the training and admonition of the Lord."
3. **Psalm 127:3** - "Behold, children are a heritage from the Lord. The fruit of the womb is a reward."
4. **Luke 2:52** - "Jesus grew in wisdom and in stature and in favour with God and all the people."
5. **Deuteronomy 11:18-19** - "So commit yourselves wholeheartedly to these words of mine. Tie them to your hands and wear them on your forehead as reminders. Teach them to your children. Talk about them when you are at home and when you are on the road; when you are going to bed and when you are getting up."
6. **Psalm 112:1-2** - "Blessed is the man who fears the Lord, who delights greatly in His commandments. His descendants will be mighty on earth; the generation of the upright will be blessed."
7. **Luke 6:40** - "A disciple is not above his teacher, but everyone who is perfectly trained will be like his teacher."
8. **3 John 1:4** - "I have no greater joy than to hear that my children walk in truth."
9. **Proverbs 10:1** - "A wise son makes a glad father; but a foolish son is the grief of his mother."
10. **Proverbs 1:8-9** - "Hear, my son, your father's instruction, and forsake not your mother's teaching; for they are graceful garland for your head and pendants for your neck."
11. **Colossians 3:21** - "Fathers, do not embitter your children, or they will become discouraged."

12. **Hebrews 12:11** - *"No discipline seems pleasant at the time, but painful. Later on, however, it produces a harvest of righteousness and peace for those who have been trained by it."*
13. **Proverbs 13:24** - *"Whoever spares the rod hates their children, but the one who loves their children is careful to discipline them."*
14. **Proverbs 29:15** - *"A rod and a reprimand impart wisdom, but a child left undisciplined disgraces his mother."*
15. **Proverbs 29:17** - *"Discipline your children, and they will give you peace; they will give you the delights your desire."*
16. **Proverbs 1:8-9** - *"Listen, my son, to your father's instructions and do not forsake your mother's teaching. They are a garland to grace your head and a chain to adorn your neck."*
17. **Hebrews 12:7-10** - *"Endure hardship as discipline; God is treating you as His children. For what children are not disciplined by their father? If you are not disciplined, and everyone undergoes discipline, then you are not legitimate, not true sons and daughters at all. Moreover, we have all the human fathers who disciplines us, and we respect them for it. How much more should we submit to the Father of spirits and live! They disciplined us for a while as they thought best, but God disciplines us for our good, in order that we may share in His holiness."*
18. **Proverbs 3:1-12** - *"My son, do not forget my teaching but keep my commands in your heart, for they will prolong your life many years and bring you peace and prosperity. Let love and faithfulness never leave you; bind them around your neck, write them on the tablet of your heart. Then you will win favour and a good name in the sight of God and man. Trust in the Lord with all your heart and lean not on your own understanding. In all your ways submit to Him and He will make your paths straight. Do not be wise in your own eyes, fear the Lord and shun evil. This will bring health to your body and nourishment to your bones.......My son, do not despise the Lord's discipline, and*

*do not resent His rebuke because the Lord disciplines those He loves, as a father the son He delights in."*

From the cited scriptural references (especially the last one), it is quite apparent that God expects parenting to adequately reflect the fear of God and NOT earthly fear. And because God is love, according to I John 4:16-18, God wants parents to inculcate the spirit of love while training and raising their children. Hear and listen to what John said in the above quote: *"And we have known and believed the love that God has for us. God is love and he who abides in love abides in God, and God in Him. Love has been perfected among us in this; that we may have boldness in the day of judgement, because as He is, so are we in this world. There is no fear in love, but perfect love casts out fear, because fear involves torment. But he who fears has not been made perfect in love."* Reflecting the image and likeness of God means that we must be able to show level-headedness, be fearless, full of power, and be able to showcase signs and wonders at all times.

Parenting is extremely powerful because it directly correlates to the actions, attitudes and overall behaviour of the children we are trying to raise. The effect can be positive or negative, depending on our background and the foundational training (or parenting) we received growing up. And that reminds me of a very popular saying, "You cannot give what you don't have!" In one way or another, our lives and attitudes would unavoidably reflect the nature, behaviour and character of those who raised us, whether we like it or not. It might not be 100%, but it would be above 50%! In Africa, most children live with and are trained by an uncle, aunty or relative; hence those tendencies could be instilled even from non-biological parents. This is why a parent has the most formative influence on a child's life.

For this reason, children are not equipped to raise themselves because they find guidance elsewhere if their biological parents are incapable of training or parenting them. That is why parents who usually put their children in daycare centres, under baby seaters or are influenced by house-maids, MUST continually assess their children's character and behaviour after returning from those places to ensure the child has not deviated from the norm being taught at home! All in all, parenting strategies should involve the following:

1. **Navigating through their feelings**
2. **Motivating them to join a noble cause**
3. **Discussing important and current events around the world so that they may be conscious of their environment**
4. **Teaching them to say "Thank you"**
5. **Teaching them to be role models**
6. **Teaching them how to be caring**
7. **Creating time for leisure, because like they always say, "All work and no plan makes Jack (and Jill) a dull boy!"**

# 7

# Do You Want to be a Good Parent?

Being a good parent can be challenging, but it could also be the most fulfilling thing a parent could ever do.

We must love God, teach them the truth about His word, and be godly examples by committing ourselves to His commands. We must emphasize the contents of Deuteronomy 6:6-7 to them, which says: *"And these words which I command you today shall be in your heart. You shall teach them diligently to your children and shall talk of them when you sit at home, when you walk by the way, when you lie down and when you rise up."* Biblical truth should be the foundation of our homes. By following the principles of these commands, we teach our children that worshipping God should be regular and MUST not be done on Sundays only or during our evening devotional hours.

According to Ephesians 5:21, which says, *"Submitting to one another in the fear of God."* Husbands and wives must be mutually respectful and very careful in all they do because our children see us as the best role models. We must realize that Jesus Christ is the Head of every man, while the man is the head of the woman, though the latter MUST not be treated or handled like a slave or second-class citizen. The wife should, however, be very submissive to her husband for peace to reign in their home. The husband's responsibility as the head of the household is to openly love his wife as he loves his own body, in the sacrificial way that Jesus Christ loved His church, according to Ephesians 5:25-29. Once the wife affirms her husband's loving leadership, she will not find it difficult to submit to his authority (according to Ephesians 5:24 and Colossians 3:18). The main responsibility is to love and respect her husband, live in wisdom and purity, and effectively take care of the home (Titus 2:4-5). Let us bear it in mind that women are naturally woven to be more nurturing than men because their sole responsibility is to be the primary caretakers of the children.

Discipline and giving godly instructions to children are integral aspects of being a good and godly parent, according to Proverbs 13:24 *"He who acres the rod hates his son, but he who loves him is careful to discipline him."* It should be noted that children who grow up in undisciplined households usually feel unwanted and unworthy. As they grow older, they lack direction and self-control, become rebellious and have little or no respect for any constituted authority. The Bible enjoins us in the book of Proverbs 19:18 to *"Discipline your son, for in that there is hope; do not be a willing party to his death."* However, the act of disciple must not erase transparent love; otherwise, such children would become resentful and discouraged (Colossians 3:21). As mentioned earlier in Hebrews 12:11, God recognizes that discipline is usually seen to be unpalatable while it is being enforced.

Let me pause to give a practical example of what this scriptural reference implies. It happened to our second son. While in secondary school, he was fond of stretching his legs on the sofa in our living room. On such occasions, his mother would caution him to "immediately bring down his legs." And he complied. However, many years later, after he had married and settled down, both his mom and I visited him in his apartment. While relaxing in his living room, he deliberately raised his legs and kept them on the table as he did many years before, perhaps to taunt his mom! Obviously aware of his expectations, his mom said nothing, and he now said, "But mom, you didn't even say anything?" Her response? "Oh, I can't complain or control you because you're now in your own house, and you can do whatever pleases you here!"

Nurturing and training a child's conscience to focus on God, avoid sin, and the common sinful nature of mankind is another primary function of a godly and responsible parent. We should train children in a godly way, planning deliberately, purposefully and consciously to raise them with the fear of God. Godly children don't come by default or accidentally. They are products of the efforts of committed godly parents. In this process, offspring of such a foundation is taught to live right and are prayerful. Fasting and praying at will would not be strange to them, and ultimately godliness and righteousness become their norm. For this reason, young couples must be ready and qualified for parenthood before marriage!

As I mentioned earlier, one can not give what he doesn't have. That is why parents who know the way ought to show it to their children so that they can grow into fruitful, productive adults who can reflect the likeness of Jesus Christ-His nature, character and behaviour in their lives. Parenting must be properly planned and intentional. It must also be focused and have an expected end from the beginning.

Parenting has a lot to do with one's background and upbringing. That is why Adam produced children and descendants in his own likeness and image! As parents, we are all sinners, but we must encourage our children NOT to commit wilful sins and be encouraged not to tell lies or be jealous unnecessarily. Since children usually return to the values, beliefs, and training they receive from their parents; parents should endeavour as much as possible to begin the conscious training of the children from birth through to age 7, as 7 is the figure of perfection, rest and completeness. And since we are spiritual beings housed in physical bodies, our spiritual bodies are ageless. Hence, when we train our children, it goes straight into their spiritual bodies, taking root and beginning to grow. Children cannot raise themselves, which is why we should be intentional about their health, success, and welfare. Many parents leave their children to fend for themselves without knowing how unsafe this practice is. Why? Most children become depressed, rebellious and suicidal because their parents abandoned them to their fate to look after themselves. Such children join delinquent groups, gangs, and secret cults and engage in other negative tendencies. They inevitably find themselves in avoidable problems, putting their parents and families in serious and unpalatable issues.

Understandably, economic demands and realities make it compelling for both the father and mother to seek employment within the government sector. Their job demands usually take a serious toll on the amount of time they spend monitoring and training their children, leaving older siblings with the onerous tasks of looking after their younger ones while the parents are at work. This is unsafe! Such parents must always double-check their children's behaviour regularly to see if they have deviated from the norm.

We need to intimately discuss other "tenets" of godly parenting by good parents at this juncture.

Parents must love their children equitably. Jacob failed to do this, and openly demonstrated how much more he loved Joseph than his siblings by sewing him a special coat of many colours. Additionally, the way Joseph handled his dream and its interpretation where his siblings and even his parents would one day bow down before him caused very serious acrimony within the family. But for God and in fulfilment of Joseph's assigned destiny, he would have missed the golden opportunity to excel in life! This is why parents must openly avoid favouritism and preferential treatment while raising and training their children. Joseph was thrown into the pit after being sold into slavery by his brothers. They later told their parents that he had died; as evidenced by his garment that they smeared with the blood of an animal His brothers lied to their father while becoming hard, mean, and embittered toward him. Imagine the vast problems that befell the family as a result of simply loving one son more than the others! Godly parents must never allow such a scenario to play out in their families. I encourage you to patiently read the full account of the story in Genesis 37-50.

The welfare of the children we train today will ultimately reflect in the lives of future generations because whatever we deposit into a thing is what we shall obviously reap as dividends! Thus, the quality of our parenting today will be reflected in our children's lives, values, behaviour, and character. And they will, in turn, unavoidably reproduce the same in the lives of their own children. Our success or failure will have long-term consequences on the overall wellness of our children. That is why we must train them carefully, deliberately, intentionally and adequately with the fear of God to reflect love, kindness, service for God and humanity, and the ability to live a sinless life. Many parents have formed the conscious habit of making empty threats toward their children. They believe in their purest hearts by threatening "to beat," "break the heads," or even "deal with" their children if they dared to commit a particular offence will suffice. Once such an offence is committed, and the parent fails to do what they threatened to carry out, their children will eventually refuse to take them seriously. That is how doubts and carefree attitudes begin to rule the lives of such children. They tend to become rebellious concerning their parents and instructions; that is the truth!

Parents should therefore be wise, practical and realistic in their choice of words while dealing with children. Apart from the implications of the weight of the words, Proverbs 18:21 reminds us that *"The power of life and death is in the tongue,"* and *"As a man thinketh, so is he"* according to Proverbs 23:7! 2 Corinthians 12:14 says, *"Behold…….for the children ought not to lay up for the parents, but the parents for the children."* Meaning? Good and responsible parents are expected to provide every need and requirement that will enable their children to live a comfortable life. They must never allow their children to assume, believe or conclude that they are living a double standard. They should concern themselves with their child's welfare regularly. Parents are encouraged to deliberately interact with their children in things such as sports, activities in school, the friends they move or interact with, health, aspirations and plans for the future and how NOT to keep malice.

That is why parents should try to always have a good rapport with their children by being patient, listening and being sensitive c to their wants, and NEVER shunning them. Some parents are very fond of saying, "Don't disturb me. Go and meet your mom; I am busy." The moment this becomes frequent, it usually pushes children to find emergency fathers or mothers outside the home because they no longer have faith in their parents nor see them as someone they could trust or confide in. Not only is this unsafe, but it is equally dangerous for the child's future and, by extension, their own children.

That is why the child's spiritual growth far outweighs their physical development. Children require patience, guidance, clearly defined limits or boundaries, and consistent discipline to genuinely mould them to become wonderful ambassadors of the family wherever they are.

Children must feel secure with their parents, and see them as semi-gods. They should be able to feel secure while growing up without fear, anxiety, psychological torture or spiritual problems. Their behaviours and general characteristics usually reveal and reflect the type of training they had while growing up.

Undoubtedly, children who lack proper parental training or care are easily discernible by how they dress, speak, and overall appearance.

Their future could begin to go down the drain, causing them to associate with persons who would give them bad ideas that could manipulate them into offence, smoking, and other dangerous drugs. Such children eventually begin to suffer depression and become dropouts and potential liabilities to society. They would have nothing to show for their existence on earth, thus making their parents ashamed of them.

Since children learn to socialize and relate to other people properly while playing with each other, it is better to create time and an avenue for them to relax, unwind and mix with their peers, but with great monitoring at all times. Children must not be over-tasked with engagements or commitments that far outweigh their capabilities, strength or ability. It is therefore advisable to give them age-related responsibilities and activities that increase based on their abilities as they grow older.

Parents must not cheat or allow their children to realize that they tell lies but be truthful and plain before them. Promises made must be kept, and every pledge should be redeemed. Ephesians 6:1-3 says, *"Children, obey your parents in the Lord, for this is right. Honour thy father and mother (which is the first commandment with promise), that it may be well with thee; and thou mayest live long on the earth."* Thus, while parents have their own roles to play, children also have to be submissive to the authority of their parents, as there are always two sides to every coin or currency. Children must respect and honour their parents because of the inherent blessings.

Apart from providing for their physical needs, the primary responsibility of parents is to train their children to know and love God, according to Deuteronomy 6:4-9 *"Hear, O Israel: The Lord our God, the Lord is one! You shall love the Lord your God with all your heart, with all your soul, and with all your strength. And these words which I command you today shall be in your heart. You shall teach them diligently to your children, and shall talk of them when you sit in your house, when you walk by the way, when you lie down and when you rise up……. You shall write them on the doorposts of your house and on your gates."*

Parental responsibilities include the legal rights, duties, powers and authority a parent has for the child and the child's property. As a good steward of the children that God has put in their care, a godly parent has the responsibility to openly care for their children's spiritual, emotional, and physical well-being at all times. Such training should reflect Jesus Christ both in action and in word. Through proper guidance and constant reminders, parents are encouraged to help their children to spend their time judiciously and deliberately support their desires to learn new things, in and out of school. Godly parents must carefully notice what their children love to do, as it might be a signal to their career path!

As much as practicable, parents must acknowledge their children's efforts in whatever they do. Correction of mistakes and errors should be done with love and without condemning their efforts in the first place. Parents must avoid statements such as, "What type of rubbish is this?" as this could kill their spirits in the future. Instead, you now say, "Oh, this is lovely; but you can do it in a better way, like this." That's a far better way to build their confidence level, where they can now gladly aspire to make another effort in future. And believe me, they would attempt to do that thing better. Children should be allowed to solve problems on their own to test their ability whenever the parent is not around. Children always tend to be curious so don't hide anything from them. Instead, teach them to be transparent. As mentioned earlier, parents must build the foundation for success in their children's hearts; hence they should be given commensurate tasks, duties and assignments. Parents should show empathy towards their children and ensure that they monitor their academic performances. Godly parents must never withhold praises and encouragement from their children whenever they do anything worthy of encouragement and accolades. The children's brains must be constantly stimulated for them to work optimally. That is why criticisms of whatever the child does must be constructive.

It is always an illusion for most of us to believe that we own children. Parents are better advised to know that children belong to God, based on Ezekiel 18:4 *"Behold, all souls are mine; as the soul of the father, so also the soul of the son is mine."* This is further reinforced in psalm 24:1 *"The earth and everything in it, the world and its inhabitants, belong to the Lord."*

The truth is, parents, can experience great joy and sorrow because of their children, according to Proverbs 10:1 *"A wise son makes a glad father; but a foolish son brings grief to his mother."* Parents must let go as their children begin to grow, according to Genesis 2:24 *"Therefore a man will leave his father and his mother and will join with his wife, and they will be one flesh."* Parents are stewards, but just because we don't own our children does not mean we don't have responsibility for their well-being. If we are duty-bound to care for something we don't own, then we are a manager or steward! Thus, if our primary responsibility as a parent is to be good stewards of our children, we need to treat the position with the reverence it is due. God has very high standards for stewards and will hold us accountable!

Since children who feel good act good, treating our children with gentleness helps them remain responsive to instructions and corrections. The Bible says in Colossians 3:21 *"Fathers, don't provoke your children so that they won't be discouraged."* It is further supported by Galatians 6:1 *"Brothers, even if a man is caught in some fault, you who are spiritual must restore such a one in a spirit of gentleness; looking to yourself so that you don't become tempted."* We must therefore handle our children tenderly. We must ensure that their five basic needs are constantly in place-life, care, control, purpose and happiness. If one or more of these needs are not being met, the child will spend a lot of energy and activity to get these needs at all costs. Parents should realize that the most important thing we need in raising a child is a relationship. Why? The relationship we have with our children is the most critical element of parenting. The value of our connection determines how well they listen to us, cooperate, and accept our limits and values.

Parenting provides the conditions in which a child can realize their full potential. Our relationship with our children, while they are growing up, will ultimately determine our future relationships with them. Hence, if we have a healthy relationship based on trust, empathy, respect and compassion, we have set a good standard. Any relationship anchored on intimidation, negative correction, coercion, or fear sets the standard relatively low and deems this relationship acceptable. Thus in order to deliberately build a great relationship, parents must do the following with their children:

1. **Spend quality time together**
2. **Be a good listener**
3. **Be trustworthy and keep every promise made**
4. **Show compassion and empathy rather than brushing off emotions that make us uncomfortable**
5. **Be an encourager and a light reflection**
6. **Apply positive discipline and respect their opinions or views**

Family culture is the family experience parents create. It is a complex blend of beliefs, attitudes, values, habits, traditions, etc. The family culture the parent creates is essentially the world in which our children are raised and profoundly shapes who they become. Parenting, therefore, requires that we find the balance between loving our children, disciplining them, and allowing them the necessary confusion and suffering that is essential for their self-discovery.

# 8

# The 10 Major Ingredients

As parents, our most valuable assets are our children, and yet so often out of our own deeds and desires, we forget that they are their own unique people. Out of good intentions and sometimes our own unresolved issues, we can become controlling or coercive, robbing our children of the freedom they need for their growth. All children have some very basic needs, which when given in the correct balance and dosage, help them to develop the resilience required for a strong sense of self. Permit me to call them the "Ten (10) Commandments of Child Growth" as discussed hereunder:

1. **Love:** All children expect and deserve to be loved adequately. We can give our children too many "things" and award them "pleasures" that they do not deserve, but these pleasures only serve to make them feel empty if they are not rightfully earned. When we love with "things," we raise entitled children with low capabilities to experience lasting joy. We love them because love is what they deserve, and one thing that we can never give too much of to our children is transparent and genuine love. And love is very simple, nonmaterial, and gives our children complete acceptance.

2. **Faith:** Raising children is very scary, and as parents, we can get so caught up in fear if we forget to quickly activate our faith. Our belief in our children determines their belief in themselves. Therefore, when our children feel dominated by our fears about every little thing they want to do, explore or experience, our fears covertly communicate that we do not believe in them. This covert message undermines our children, causing them to either not believe in themselves or rebel against our fears' controlling nature. So as parents, we must have faith in our children and give them the rope they need to struggle, discover, and succeed.

3. **Confidence:** Once our children can safely confirm that we have confidence in them, they become naturally confident in themselves. On the other hand, if we behave contentiously towards them, showing a lack of trust in their character, or the ability to make wise decisions, we go against them, putting us on different ends of the spectrum. As parents, we must accept that our children are different and unique people from us. We should allow them the space to be different and trust that we have raised them well enough to make mistakes, recover, and do better next time. If we respond contentiously to their mistakes or decisions, we slowly crush their own drives for self-improvement.

4. **Patience:** Obviously, parenting is a challenging task because we have an idea of what we think is the best for our children, and can over-pressure them to be the image we hold of them. However, our children require our patience, NOT our pressure. They expect us to give them a little rope to come along at their own pace. Each child develops on their own unique course, and if they are not on par in every area of life, adding pressure and control only defeats them. With patience and enough time, they will find their way. Once we attempt to pressure them, we will kill their spirits and motivation. We must not deliberately raise children who only feel loved if they are performing because they are not perfect.

5. **Attention:** Touch is one of the most important and grounding aspects of a relationship. Touch cures our hormones for bonding, love and a sense of security. It has also been shown to have an immediate impact on reducing stress levels. Our children could go through the same hell as any other human being. When we see them struggling, it is not helpful for us to heap our own anxieties about their struggle on them. We, therefore, need to offer affection and support, letting them know that "this too shall pass." A little affection is that spoonful of sugar that helps lessens and dissipates their pain. We should therefore endeavour to talk to our children, love and snuggle them, and refrain from shouting at them.

6. **Counsel:** One of the major roles of parents is to provide feedback that is conducive to building their character. Their growth could easily suppress when we criticize, yell, berate or become passive-aggressive. They will shrink and could become enraged and develop negative feelings about themselves, their capabilities, and us. When we rob our children of their pain and do not give them room for failure, we also rob them of their pursuit of happiness. Our children need our genuine counsel to understand that the most important part of life is the worthwhile struggle to discover a great sense of meaning and purpose.

7. **Compassion:** Parents must never forget that each child is their own person. They are not here to be like us, even though that is the conscious expectation of some parents. They are not in this world to be as good as or better than their siblings, peers, or our friends' children. Whenever we compare our children, we are telling them that they are not good enough. This can seriously undermine motivation and make them feel a lack of their own significance. There is no comparison at all. We can only compare someone to themselves, and despite that, we all occasionally have our low moments in life, which we always wish to move on from. However, if we decide to compare, it should only be

done to show how far our children have come from where they were before. It is always better to use compassion instead of comparison.
8. **Guidance:** It is our role to teach our children right from wrong, but it is not our right to decide who they are supposed to be. As parents, we need to stay away from controlling, manipulating and pulling our children away from their natural interests. We must allow them to explore their own decision-making process in lieu of making decisions for them. Once we show disgust or disappointment over their choices because they are not the choices we would have made, it then becomes manipulation. To be great leaders, we need to live the lives we love to have a purpose beyond our children. We must not live our lives and unrealized dreams through our children, as it is not their responsibility to make up for what we are missing in our own lives.
9. **Respect:** If we fail to respect our children, they will, in turn, learn not to respect us as parents. Children tend to do as we do and not as we say. They are not going to respect us simply because we are adults. They usually respect the adults who respect them. If you ridicule them, they will ridicule and disobey the parent. If you want to be respected by them, parents should respect themselves and show them what it looks like. Most importantly, it is advisable to respect them because they naturally learn to respect themselves and their parents through the reciprocal respect given to them. If a parent is emotionally immature and rage, ridicule and ignore their children, they indirectly teach them how to respond to them and live in the same manner.
10. **Time:** As parents, our children need our love, time and utmost attention. Nobody can effectively substitute us. We must not allow video games, babysitters, iPads or other things to take our place in our children's lives. Nothing should be allowed to be our children's caretaker. We are all working in a society which has its own obligations, but our children must be given priority.

Parents should make time to spend with their children daily in whatever capacity that they can to appropriate to their developmental level. Whenever our children are in need, they should be assured of our availability.

# 9

# Avoid These as Much as Possible

Since the commencement of this book, we have discussed most of the things that parents are expected to do. I have, however, intentionally decided to bring the following phrases to your attention. These should be avoided as much as possible and replaced with the suggested ones.

1. **"I am proud of you"**: We should not give our children a blanket statement of encouragement because the child may begin to feel responsible for parental pride. Also, by saying so in the presence of other siblings who might not have been doing well to deserve such an accolade, the parent could indirectly be sowing envy, resentment, animosity or hatred in the hearts of those to whom such praises were not given. A better way of saying it could be "Good for you."
2. **"Good job"**: Love what they did? It is far more helpful in terms of encouragement and building self-esteem if parents focus on how the child achieved whatever they accomplished. It is better to say any of these: "You got all A's, you must have worked really hard" or "I like the way you passed the ball that made your team win."

3. **"You should set a good example for your brother"**: Older siblings can act out perhaps out of jealousy due to the extra attention a younger sibling may be receiving. "Your brother looks up to you; you're such a good role model."

4. **"I will never forgive you"**: This phrase is very common among parents but should be avoided as much as possible. We usually react sharply when a child does something unthinkable. Saying something like this repeatedly to a child could truly damage them. Such a child could feel that whatever he has done will forever be remembered against him, and it could cause low morale and self-esteem. Instead, we could say this: "What you did was harmful, but we will find a way to leave this behind us and carry on."

5. **"I am ashamed of you"**: Using this phrase against a child may permanently make that child feel like a disgrace in the family. Try to say this instead, "Although I feel bad about what you did, I always love who you are."

6. **"Don't cry"**: It's important to encourage children to express their emotions and not bottle them up. Help them to recognize their feelings and deal with them openly and honestly. Say something like this instead, "I know you're sad that that thing happened, but don't worry."

7. **"I am disappointed in you"**: Whatever the child might have done to upset the parent, making such a blunt statement could leave the child to feel like they have lost a loving place in the parent's eyes! It is better to say, "I'm surprised and was not expecting this to occur."

8. **"Come here, NOW"**: It is always better to give a child time to respond to our wishes instead of constantly rushing. It is better to say, "It's almost time to go. Do you want one or two minutes more?"

9. **"This is terrible, the worst"**: When things go wrong in life, a parent's constant repetition of a phrase like this could set

children on edge and cause even more concerns. By repeatedly saying fearful and emotional words, very young children may believe that the event being referred to has happened many times over! It's better to say, "I'm having a hard time believing such a tragedy, but we will talk about it if you like to."

10. **"You're stupid and good for nothing"**: Whether parents, believe it or not, harsh and negative statements such as this are prevalent among parents. They could be very detrimental to a child who hears such phrases regularly. Instead, parents could say: "Oh, look at what you did" or "Don't repeat such a thing next time."

In addition to the above, parents who sincerely love their children and expect them to live a life fashioned after Jesus Christ must always strive to take note of avoiding the following concerning their children:

1. **Ignore their brain:** Their brain controls how they think, behave, and relate to others. When it functions right, they work right. If it doesn't, they automatically have trouble in life, which would inevitably affect the parents.
2. **Rare quality time with them:** Relationships require special time. The most effective exercise a parent can do is spend 20 minutes of quality time a day with the child, listening and doing something they want to do for cogent reasons.
3. **Be a poor listener:** We should be good listeners by always allowing our children the opportunity to fully express themselves, instead of ignoring or interrupting them. This gives them joy and the courage to see their parents as a dependable source of their challenges and dissuades them from relying on outside sources that might mislead them in future.
4. **Use name calling:** Parents must not tell their child, "You're a spoiled brat." This is not helpful and can cause children to internalize these negative names and eventually believe them.

5. **Be overly permissive:** Allowing our children to do whatever they want may make them "happy" in the short run but can be detrimental in the long run. Children should be given very clear boundaries. Parents must be firm because children who have the most psychological problems usually have parents who do not set boundaries.
6. **Fail to supervise them:** Parents must constantly check in on what their children are doing from time to time and with whom they are doing what. It shows that such a parent cares.
7. **Do as I say, not as I do:** If the parent is a poor role model, their children are more than likely to pick up on that and follow the parent's lead. For example, if the parent keeps telling the child to eat plenty of fruits, and the parent is not openly doing so, such a child will likely opt for the foods they see the parent eat instead of the fruit their parent is encouraging them to eat.
8. **Only notice what they do wrong:** As much as possible, parents should try to notice when their children do things that they admire and comment on them. Adults and grown-ups equally love to be appreciated and given a pat on the back. Parents must NOT only see the shortfalls or the mistakes of their children.
9. **Ignore their mental health issues:** Godly and loving parents must be able to monitor the mental alertness of their children regularly. It is almost the same as item "A" above, where we spoke about the child's brain. How fast does the child respond to issues? Is the response reasonable? How does he contribute to discussions? Are such contributions meaningful?
10. **Ignore your own mental health:** If the parent is suffering from a mental health condition, it can devastate the child. Thus, according to a popular saying that says, "Put your own oxygen mask on first," the parent should take care of himself first in order to be able to efficiently look after the home front with proper and sound supervision, especially over the children.

Thus, any parent that loves their children, and wants them to grow into stable, thoughtful, productive, loving adults, must AVOID doing any of the above to their children.

Children are truly a blessing from God, but they don't come with an instruction manual. However, there is no better place to find cogent advice on parenting than from the best manual in the world- the Bible. It reveals a Heavenly Father who loves and calls us His children. It contains enormous examples of godly parents. It gives direct, Christ-driven and straightforward instructions on how to parent effectively and efficiently. It is also filled with many principles that can be applied to become the best parents ever.

# 10

# Special Biblical References on Child Training & Parenting

**Fear the Lord:** Proverbs 1:7 *"The fear of the Lord is the beginning of wisdom."* Ultimately, parenting is not about teaching the right behaviours; it is about facilitating the right relationship. As a parent, our first assignment is to help our children relate to God through faith in Jesus Christ so that they can be reconciled to God through the life and death of Jesus Christ.

**Revere God's word:** Proverbs 2:6 *"For the Lord gives wisdom; from His mouth come knowledge and understanding."* Also, Proverbs 13:13 says, "Whoever despises the word brings destruction on himself, but he who reveres the Commandments will be rewarded." Parents must teach their children the commandments of God. Not as a means of salvation but as a path of wisdom, life and fruitfulness. We must show them how much we value the Word of God. They should be able to see that we read our Bible regularly and meditate on it. Parents build their lives on the unchanging Word of God.

**Honour the Lord:** Proverbs 3:9-10 *"Honour the Lord with your wealth and with the first fruits of all your produce; then your barns will be filled plenty, and your vats will be bursting with wine."* Parents should teach their children about generosity, faithfulness and regular giving. Let them know that money, success, and every good thing ultimately comes from God because nobody can make or promote themselves without Him. They should be taught that God gave us/them the gifts, talents, plus the opportunities that enable us to make or have what we possess, not on our own or by our power.

**Appreciate correction:** Proverbs 3:11-12 *"My son, do not despise the Lord's discipline or be weary of His reproof, for the Lord reproves him whom He loves, as a Father the Son in whom He delights."* Since a godly parent does not want to raise stupid children, they should teach their children to appreciate the many benefits of discipline. Discipline lovingly points us in the direction of peace and harmony and should be seen as a lifelong exercise. Even Proverbs 12:1 says, *"Whoever loves discipline loves knowledge, but he who hates reproof is stupid."*

**Pursue a Godly spouse:** Proverbs 12:4 *"An excellent wife if the crown of her husband, but she who brings shame is like rottenness in his bones." "Any man who finds a wife finds a good thing and obtains favour from the Lord"* Proverbs 18:22, and still from the book of Proverbs 21:9, the Bible says, *"It is better to live in a corner of the housetop than in a house shared with a quarrelsome wife."* Thus, a good spouse is a gift from God. A bad spouse is like inescapable cancer. Parents must therefore encourage their children to choose their spouse wisely and carefully.

**Learn self-control:** In Proverbs 6:32, the father speaks frankly to his son about the dangers of sexual immorality. *"He who commits adultery lacks sense; he who does it destroys himself." "Keep your way far from her, and* *do not go near the door of her house"* - Proverbs 5:8. Proverbs 21:17 also says, *"Whoever loves pleasure will be a poor man; he who loves wine and oil will not be rich."* Parents must warn their children about self-control and how to set boundaries. Children must be encouraged to have discipline regarding sex and alcohol.

**Tell the truth:** Proverbs 28:13 *"Whoever conceals his transgressions will not prosper, but he who confesses and forsakes them will obtain mercy."* Children need to learn that the best way through any problem is always by telling the truth. Thus, parents do their children no favours when covering for their mistakes. Holding on to sin in our hearts is a recipe for spiritual and psychological indigestion. Deception is a short-sighted strategy in business and the realm of personal relationships.

**Build strong relationships:** Proverbs 27:10 *"Do not forsake your friends and your father's friend, and do not go to your Brother's house in the day of your calamity. Better is a neighbour who is near, than a brother who is far away."* Parents must advise their children to build a rich, thick, multigenerational community of friends in the place where they live. They will be the people who will be readily available to carry them when they fall or need immediate assistance in case of any emergency, not the brother or the sibling in another country. So, children must be taught to value relationships and friendships.

**Work hard, don't be lazy:** Proverbs 10:4-5 *"A slack hand causes poverty, but the hand of the diligent makes rich."* Wise parents point their children toward a productive enterprise, help them make the connection between labour and increase, and help them develop the skills necessary to provide for a family and contribute to the community. Parents should teach their children that work comes before play, how to work hard and make hay while the sun shines.

**Show mercy to the poor:** Proverbs 14:31 *"Whoever oppresses a poor man insults his Maker, but he who is generous to the needy honours Him."* Children must be taught how to treat all human beings with dignity. They should also honour God by being generous to the needy. Even James 1:27 says, *"Religion that is pure and undefiled before God the Father is this: to visit Orphans and Widows in their affliction and to keep oneself untainted from the world."* Holiness and charity go hand in hand. Parents should teach their children to be merciful to the poor.

I strongly encourage you, my reader, to read this outgoing chapter as often as possible and apply the inherent principles in parenting your children. Sunday school teachers, spouses and students should also adhere to the contents and put them to practice as practicable as possible.

# 11

# Children and Their Parents

Having a child is like having one's heart walking around outside of the body. As any parent knows, the process of raising a child is rich with emotions, uncertainties, joys and sorrows.

Let me share some very cogent scriptures that are very apt concerning parenting and children:

1. **Isaiah 54:13** - *"All your children shall be taught by the Lord, and great shall be the peace of your children."*
2. **Proverbs 1:8-9** - *"Hear, my son, your father's instruction and forsake not your mother's teaching, for they are a garland for your head and pendants for your neck."*
3. **Matthew 19:14** - *"Jesus said, let little children come to me, and do not hinder them, for the Kingdom of God belongs to such as these."*
4. **Proverbs 17:6** - *"Children's children are a crown to the aged, and parents are the pride of their children."*

5. **3 John 1:4** - *"I have no greater joy than to hear that my children are walking in the truth."*
6. **Deuteronomy 5:29** - *"Oh, that their hearts would be inclined to fear me and keep all my commands always, so that it might go well with them and their children forever."*
7. **Matthew 18:1-3** - *"At that time the Disciples come to Jesus saying, "Who is the greatest in the Kingdom of Heaven?" And calling to Him a child, he put him in the midst of them and said, "Truly, I say to you, unless you turn and become like children, you will never enter the Kingdom of Heaven."*
8. **Psalm 139:15-16** - *"My frame was not hidden from you when I was made in the secret place, when I was woven together in the depths of the earth. Your eyes saw my unformed body; all the days ordained for me were written in your book before one of them came to be."*
9. **Colossians 3:21** - *"Father's, do not embitter your children, or they will become discouraged."*
10. **Proverbs 29:15-17** - *"To discipline a child produces wisdom, but a mother is disgraced by an undisciplined child. When the wicked are in authority, sin flourishes, but the godly will live to see their downfall. Discipline your children, and they will give you peace of mind and will make your heart glad."*
11. **I Timothy 4:12** - *"Let no one despise you for your youth, but set the believers an example in speech, in conduct, in love, in faith, in purity."*
12. **Titus 2:6-7** - *"Encourage young men to use good judgment. Always set an example by doing good things. When you teach, be an example of moral purity and dignity."*
13. **I Timothy 5:8** - *"But if anyone does not provide for his relatives, and especially for members of his households, he has denied the faith and is worse than an unbeliever."*

14. **Galatians 6:10** - *"So then, as we have opportunity, let us do good to everyone, and especially to those who are of the household of faith."*
15. **Proverbs 6:20** - *"My son, keep your father's commandments, and forsake not your mother's teaching."*
16. **Proverbs 23:22-25** - *"Listen to your father who gave you life, and do not despise your mother when she is old. Buy truth, and do not sell it; buy wisdom, instruction and understanding. The father of the righteous will greatly rejoice; he who fathers a wise son will be glad in him. Let your father and mother be glad; let her who bore you rejoice."*
17. **Leviticus 19:3** - *"Every one of your shall revere his mother and his father, and you shall keep my Sabbath: I am the Lord your God."*
18. **Proverbs 17:6** - *"Grandchildren are the crown of the aged, the glory of children is their fathers."*
19. **Luke 1:46-48** - *"And Mary said, "My soul magnifies the Lord, and my spirit rejoices in God my Saviour, for He has looked on the humble estate of His servant. For behold, from now on, all generations will call me blessed."*
20. **I Samuel 1:26-28** - *"And she said, "Oh my Lord! As you live, my lord, I am the woman who was standing here in your presence, praying to the Lord. For this child I prayed, and the Lord has granted me my petition that I made to Him. Therefore, I have lent him to the Lord. As long as he lives, he is lent to the Lord. And he worshipped the Lord there."*
21. **2 Corinthians 6:18** - *"And I will be a father to you, and you shall be sons and daughters to me, says the Lord Almighty."*
22. **Hebrews 12:7** - *"It is for discipline that you have to endure. God is treating you as sons. For what son is there whom his father does not discipline?"*
23. **Luke 11:11-12** - *"What father among you, if his son asks for a fish, will instead of a fish give him a serpent; or if he asks for an egg, will give him a scorpion?"*

24. **Proverbs 23:24** - *"The father of the righteous will greatly rejoice; he who fathers a wise son will be glad in him."*
25. **Luke 11:13** - *"If ye then, being evil, know how to give good gifts unto your children; how much more shall your Heavenly Father give the Holy Spirit to them that ask Him?"*

# *Conclusion*

Having come this far, permit me to conclude with a summary of the following duties of a responsible parent:

1. **To protect your children from harm**
2. **To provide your child with food, clothing and shelter**
3. **To give financial support**
4. **To effectively provide safety, supervision and control**
5. **To provide medical care**
6. **To provide education**

Raising children can be very challenging and rewarding, but good and godly parents must fulfill various roles for children to become healthy and happy people. Parents must teach moral values such as respect, responsibility, honesty, patience, compassion, forgiveness and the fear of God to their children. This is done through deliberate training, with the intention to be prominent role models to them.

Parents who profess to be good must glaringly AVOID physical, sexual and/or emotional abuse or neglect in the course of raising their children, as this is bad parenting. Good and responsible parents must be proactive and NOT reactive by encouraging their children to express themselves freely; while still properly digesting every statement from or by their children. If a child suddenly begins to misbehave, the parents must try to understand what led to it. They must still be appreciated as children, so parents must be careful in their choice of words while reprimanding them when they misbehave. Parents must also monitor their free time and interactions with their friends and peers.

Children must be encouraged to say "Thank you," "Please," "I'm sorry," "Oh, it was a mistake," or "Please forgive me" when appropriate, without any hesitation or compulsion. Children usually want to make their fathers proud, and an involved father promotes inner growth and strength. When fathers are affectionate and supportive, it dramatically affects a child's cognitive and social development and instills an overall sense of well-being and confidence.

# A Sinner's Prayer

Dear Heavenly Father,

I come to You in the Name of Jesus Christ.

You said in Your Word, "Whosoever shall call upon the name of the Lord shall be saved" (Romans 10:13). I am calling on Your Name, so I know You have saved me now.

You also said that "if you confess with your mouth the Lord Jesus and believe in your heart that God has raised Him from the dead, you will be saved. For with the heart one believes unto righteousness, and with the mouth, confession is made unto salvation" (Romans 10:9-10). I believe in my heart Jesus Christ is the Son of God. I believe that He was raised from the dead for my justification, and I confess Him now as my Lord and Savior.

Thank you, Lord, because now, I am saved!

Thank You, Lord, because I know you have heard my prayer. Thank You, Lord, because I am now born again.

Signed _____

Date _____

# About the Author

Apostle Dr. Victor Adekunle Adewusi was a passionate Spiritual Leader and Father of many children and grandchildren.

He was also the Author of five books *"The Secrets of Happy Parenting," "Control Your Anger," "Praise, Appreciation & Thanksgiving (PAT)," "Mine Shall Be Done,"* and *"Fear Not, Cheer Up, Do Not Despair."*

Until his passing, he was the General Overseer of The Eternal Sacred Order of The Cherubim and Seraphim Church, Oke Ibukun Branco; The Governor of the Yabatech Class of 1986 governing council; a Member of The Chartered Institute of Management; A Fellow of The Chartered Institute of Taxation of Nigeria and A Fellow of The Institute of Chartered Accountants of Nigeria (ICAN).

Apostle Dr. Victor Adekunle, who was a philanthropist, has drawn on his personal breakthrough life experiences to help people overcome challenges and attain greater achievements in their life.

www.ingramcontent.com/pod-product-compliance
Lightning Source LLC
Chambersburg PA
CBHW070341010526
44107CB00004B/589